Titles in the series

A SNOWY DAY
A STORMY DAY
A SUNNY DAY
A WINDY DAY

WHAT CAN I HEAR?
WHAT CAN I SEE?
WHAT CAN I TASTE?
WHAT CAN I TOUCH?

CLEAN AND DIRTY
HOT AND COLD
LIGHT AND DARK
WET AND DRY

COTTON
GLASS
RUBBER
WOOD

BEANS
BREAD
FRUIT
VEGETABLES

BREATHING
EATING
MOVING
SLEEPING

British Library Cataloguing in Publication Data
Richardson, Joy, *1948-*
Sleeping.
1. Man. Sleep
I. Title   II. Series
612.821

ISBN 0-340-53255-6

First published 1991

Published by Hodder and Stoughton Children's Books,
a division of Hodder and Stoughton Ltd,
Mill Road, Dunton Green, Sevenoaks, Kent TN13 2YA

Printed in Italy

SLEEPING

Joy Richardson

Illustrated by Polly Noakes

HODDER AND STOUGHTON
LONDON SYDNEY AUCKLAND TORONTO

'Goodnight.
Sleep tight.'

Thomas snuggles under the
covers and closes his eyes. He
feels warm and comfortable.

His brain is still busy.
'Tomorrow I'll build a den,' he
thinks, 'and make a model and...'

Slowly his thoughts get into a
muddle. Thomas is falling asleep.

Dad comes in.
He picks up teddy and
tucks him into bed. He
kisses Thomas and
turns out the light.

Thomas does not notice.
He is fast asleep.

When Thomas is awake, his
eyes and ears rush messages to
his brain for thinking about.

Sleep switches off the
brain's message receiver.
Only very strong messages
can get through.

Everyone needs sleep, but
children need more than
grown-ups.

Thomas is asleep nearly
half the time. His little
sister sleeps even more.

Children grow most
when they are asleep.

While Thomas sleeps,
his heartbeat slows down.
He breathes more slowly.
His muscles relax. He is
gathering energy for
tomorrow.

The dog needs sleep too.
He curls up in his basket.

The house is quiet
except for the hamster.
He likes to sleep in the
day and play on his
wheel at night-time.

Out in the garden birds sleep
on branches, holding tight with
their feet.

Fish sleep at the bottom of the
pond, with their eyes open.

An owl flies off in the
darkness to go hunting.
He is a night creature.

People are day creatures,
but sometimes they have
to work at night.

10

Thomas's auntie is looking after people in hospital tonight. She will work all night and go home to sleep at breakfast time.

The clock strikes midnight.
Dad is sleeping lightly. The
clock wakes him up.

Thomas is sleeping deeply.
He does not hear it.

Some people sleep so deeply
that they can walk about, or
talk in their sleep, without
waking up.

Once Thomas wet the bed.
He was so fast asleep that
he did not wake up in time.

Thomas begins to dream. He makes a very tall tower in the middle of the jungle to escape from lions. He climbs to the top, then cannot get down.

Thomas feels very frightened.
He calls out and wakes himself up.
'It's all right,' says his mum. 'It's
only a dream.'

Thomas soon goes back to sleep
and starts another dream.

When Thomas dreams his eyes jerk about beneath his eyelids. They seem to be watching the pictures inside his head.

Thomas has lots of dreams every single night. He forgets them unless he wakes up straightaway.

Most of his dreams vanish. He cannot remember having them.

Thomas's dreams are made of
bits and pieces of thoughts and
feelings, and things he has
seen and done.

His brain mixes them together
into strange stories.

Dreams refresh the brain
and help to sort it out.

The dog has dreams too
but cannot tell anyone
about them.

Thomas turns over in his sleep.
He curls up and straightens out.
He lies on his side and then
on his back.

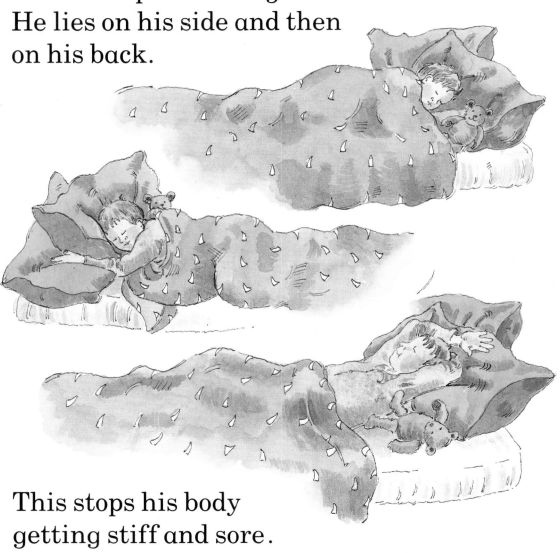

This stops his body
getting stiff and sore.

Sometimes he snores. His mouth drops open. His tongue falls back and traps air on its way in. It makes a bubbly sound.

21

Morning comes.
Thomas is sleeping lightly.
His little sister calls out.

Thomas wakes up.
His brain and his body
have had a good rest.

'Sleep is funny', he says. 'It makes tomorrow come soon.' 'Too soon,' says Mum sleepily, but Thomas is already busy with his model.

23

sleeping words

bed

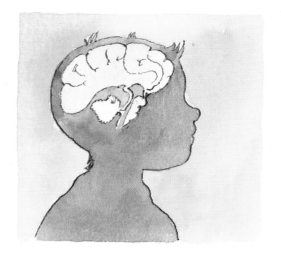

brain

dream

night night creatures

snore